This edition published in 2017 by
Carlton Books Limited, 20 Mortimer Street
London W1T 3JW

First published in 1997.

A CIP catalogue entry for this book is available from the British Library.

ISBN 978 1 78097 932 8

Printed in Dubai

3 5 7 9 10 8 6 4

DIANA
THE PEOPLE'S PRINCESS

A CELEBRATION
OF HER LIFE AND LEGACY:
20 YEARS ON

NICHOLAS OWEN
FOREWORD BY SIR TREVOR MCDONALD

CARLTON
BOOKS

CONTENTS

FOREWORD

SIR TREVOR McDONALD, OBE

The sudden and tragic death of Diana, Princess of Wales affected the people of Britain and the world as perhaps no other event in modern times.

From the Far East to the furthest western point of the Americas, from northern Europe to the Antarctic, her passing was mourned by millions who had never even met her. Her death seemed to touch the chord that unites us all as people, as members of the vast and disparate human race, as partners in the great family of nations. I have come to believe that there are several reasons why this is so. Diana had become, by the time of her death, an international superstar like no other before her. Although she was no longer married to the Prince of Wales, the heir to the British throne, her superstar status was underpinned by her royal connections. To all intents and purposes she was regarded by her millions of admirers as fully royal, and touched by that indescribable regal magic. Another reason is that she was stunningly beautiful. In an age when technology enables pictures to flatter their subject unashamedly, Diana's good looks outdid the photographer's art. As Shakespeare's Cleopatra was described, Diana's entrance into a room "beggared all description".

But there was much more. In those awful, inconsolable days after her death we came to know how the Princess of Wales was viewed by the people who had come into contact with her and by the numerous charities to which she gave so freely of her time. She had obviously made a lasting impression on them. She was perceived universally as a champion of the underdog, a Princess who was con-cerned about those less fortunate than herself, the poor and the sick, and one who was prepared to challenge the most powerful governments in the world to secure an international ban on landmines. When she met the dispossessed and the persecuted, the victims of AIDS in London, and children dying of cancer in Pakistan, she sat close to them, held their hands, touched their foreheads and their cheeks and for one brief and shining moment encouraged them to believe that they were the most cherished people in all the wide world. She

7

managed in her short life to convey the feeling that she cared, that she was on the people's side, and that she'd always be ready to descend from the heady heights of celebrity and haute couture to fight for them. To have been seen in that light by so many millions of people was an extraordinary achievement.

On hearing the news of Diana's death, the world held its breath, and in London people converged on the royal palaces in tears and disbelief to express their sorrow and to make those palaces floral monuments to her memory. There was something unique about those who poured into London to mourn Diana's death, and to queue for up to eleven hours to sign books of condolence. They came from every class, country, religion and race and seemed to represent, in the infinite variety of their cultures and backgrounds, the universality of Princess Diana's appeal.

Many of us in the media knew the Princess well. She had a great sense of humour, laughed easily and was unfailingly charming. But she could also be wilful and manipulative and was always ambivalent about how much of her royal status she wanted to use and when. Diana was no saint. She made silly mistakes and even grosser misjudgements. She was not infallible. But then neither are we. Part of her charm was her vulnerability. She was very human and it is now obvious from the many tributes to her, that she was capable of showing great humanity. When it was clear that she would never be Queen of England, Diana said, with what seems like wonderful prescience, that she wanted to be Queen of People's Hearts, The People's Princess. The response by the people to her death suggests that she achieved, in overwhelming measure, everything that she wanted to be.

The undoubted value of this book lies in the simple fact that the images it contains will never die ... the pictures of the glamorous Princess; the pictures of her with her boys, the young Princes, who she loved so much. And then there are those forever haunting images of her coffin arriving back from Paris and the panorama of scenes of her funeral on the day an entire nation stopped to pay its respects. These will be pointed at and talked about long into the twenty-first century.

They show that in her short life, marked by pinnacles of joy and depths of despair, Diana, Princess of Wales, became an icon who captured the world's imagination as no other public figure of our time.

Trevor McDonald

DIANA'S
Early Life

SHE WAS A CHEERFUL, HELPFUL CHILD, BUT NEVER A STANDOUT STUDENT ❧ HER PARENTS' BITTER DIVORCE CAST A SHADOW ON HER CHILDHOOD, BUT SHE FOUND SOLACE WITH SIBLINGS AND FRIENDS, AND SHE LOVED BEING WITH CHILDREN ❧ THEN, AT 16, SHE MET THE PRINCE OF WALES AT A SHOOTING PARTY, AND HER LIFE CHANGED FOREVER ❧

Nobody could possibly have predicted her death – the timing or the manner of it. It was shocking, unbelievable and heartbreaking. Nor could anyone have predicted what happened next. A global flood of emotion that swamped the world for days – even weeks – afterwards. We journalists and commentators tried as best we could to put into words her special appeal – her special bond with the people. It was – and is – a difficult task. So what clues were there in Diana's early years?

In his emotional and unforgettable funeral address at Westminster Abbey, Diana's brother, Earl Spencer, called her a "very British girl". Certainly, Diana had an upbringing typical of the British aristocracy. She was born Diana Frances Spencer, on July 1, 1961, the daughter of Lord and Lady Althorp. Royal connections were close. Lord Althorp was a friend of the Royal Family and a former equerry to the Queen. In fact the Spencers were direct descendants of King James I, which meant that Diana and Prince Charles were distant cousins. Home to the young Diana, her two elder

RIGHT:

Diana with her brother and childhood confidant Charles in 1967.

sisters, Sarah and Jane, and younger brother, Charles, was Park House on the Royal estate at Sandringham in Norfolk. Prince Charles's younger brothers, Andrew and Edward, were frequent visitors to the Spencer family home.

Diana's life changed dramatically at the age of six when her parents separated. Three years later she was sent away to school. Until that point she had been educated at home by the same governess who had taught her mother. Her time at Riddlesworth Hall, near Thetford in Norfolk, was made miserable initially by homesickness on the one hand and a custody battle between her parents, which her father eventually won, on the other. Eventually she settled in but it was soon clear that Diana was not going to excel in the classroom. However, she enjoyed sport and was good at it. Her headmistress at the time also remembered how Diana was "awfully sweet with the little ones" as she rose through the school. One of the aims of the Riddlesworth Hall regime was to give its girls poise and good manners and in that, as Diana's later life was to prove, the school did succeed. Ironically, Diana's childhood nickname was "Duchess" because of her composed and, even then, almost regal manner. At holiday time and at weekends, she and her brother would often travel by train together from Norfolk to visit their mother, who had remarried and moved to Sussex.

12

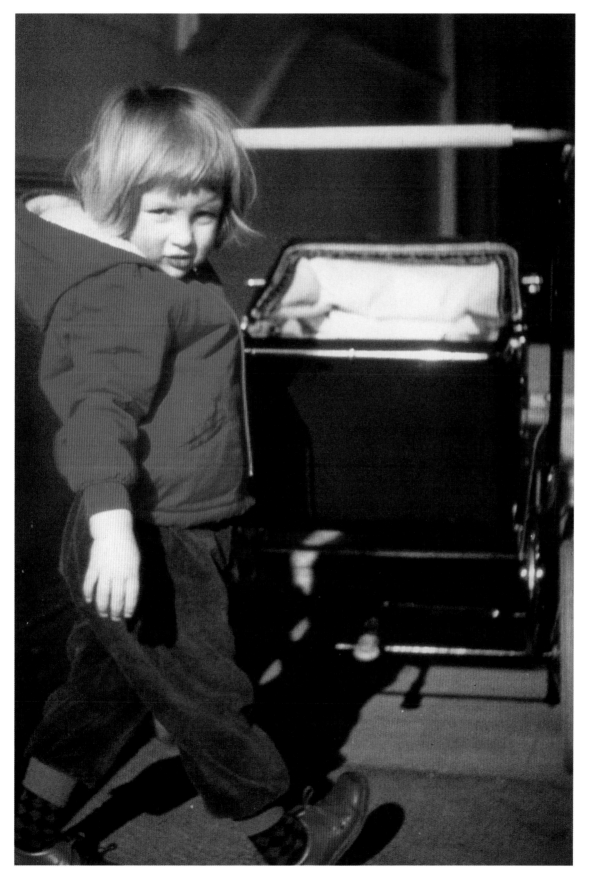

Diana in 1965.

Diana's next school was West Heath in Kent. It was here that the pin up on her dormitory wall was said to have been a picture of Prince Charles in the ceremonial robes he wore for his investiture as Prince of Wales in 1969. West Heath did not inspire any academic achievements in her either but she won prizes for swimming, developed her love of dancing both ballet and tap, and was made a prefect. One of her reports read: "She is a girl who notices what needs to be done, then does it willingly and cheerfully."

ABOVE:

It was evident when Diana was a child that the camera already loved her.

While she was at West Heath, her life was to suffer yet more upheaval. In June 1975 her grandfather died and her father succeeded him to become the eighth Earl Spencer, inheriting the family's vast ancestral mansion, Althorp in Northamptonshire. When Diana came home from West Heath at the end of the summer term of that year, Park House was being packed up for the move. She never truly became fond of Althorp, not least because of its association with another dramatic change in her family's life. Around this time, her father had become close to Raine, Countess of Dartmouth, the daughter of the novelist Barbara Cartland. In 1977 the Earl married Raine and she took charge of the estate and of the family. The Spencer children had never come across anyone like Raine before and eventually preferred to stay away from Althorp. Diana chose, whenever she could, to stay with her sisters as they had both moved to London.

In 1977, at the age of sixteen, Diana sat her major school exams – her O levels – and failed. In November that same year Diana and the Prince of Wales met for the first time when she went to a shooting party organized for Charles by her sister Sarah, who was friendly with the Prince. Years later she described Charles at that meeting as "pretty amazing" and he remembered her as "very jolly and attractive." Diana had another go at her exams that winter but still without success. Her education was supposed to end at a finishing school in Switzerland but this was not successful and she returned to England after a few weeks, suffering from homesickness. Next she completed a cookery course in Wimbledon in southwest London. Diana was

OPPOSITE:

On a family holiday in Sussex in 1970.

BELOW:

The same holiday: a barefoot Diana playing croquet.

16

OPPOSITE:

*Diana, 13, on
holiday on the
Isle of Uist.*

RIGHT:

*A family portrait:
Diana, far right,
with her father,
sisters and brother
in 1970.*

BELOW:

*A kiss for the
teenage Diana
from her Shetland
Pony, Scuffle.*

RIGHT:

Diana the
kindergarten
teacher, preparing
to become a
Princess.

living in the capital by this stage and it was now that her love of children began to reveal itself. She took nannying jobs, taught ballet to toddlers, and then became an assistant at a kindergarten – a job that she really enjoyed.

Up until this point Diana's life was much like that of many other rich young women in London. She shared a flat with three friends in a fashionable part of the city during the week and spent weekends in the country.

At the beginning of 1979 Diana and Charles met again at another shooting party and their relationship began. Initially they were friends, attending dinner parties together or taking trips to the ballet. Their relationship blossomed into a romance in the summer of 1980. That year Diana joined the Royal Family for part of their annual holiday at Balmoral Castle in Scotland. It was while they were there that the Press first found out about the relationship when they were spotted together on the estate. Diana's flatmates were as surprised as anyone when the news emerged that she was dating the heir to the throne. She had told them that the man she was going out with was called Charles Renfrew – "Baron of Renfrew" was one of Charles's many titles. When she returned to London after her holiday in Balmoral, Diana began to endure the media attention that was to trouble her until her death.

That autumn, she and Charles played a cat and mouse game with reporters, somehow managing a courtship that was at least partly private. Diana dealt with journalists calmly and discreetly, although her frequent blushes and glances from underneath her fringe quickly won her the nickname "Shy Di." It was a tough initiation for any would-be member of the Royal Family but for a nineteen-year old it was especially daunting. Charles never visited her at home. When he telephoned her he used a coded ring so she would know it was him and not one of the many journalists. Diana's flat was besieged and she was followed wherever she went. Even under this pressure, however, she somehow managed to stay calm, apart from one occasion when she broke down in tears. In a grim foretaste of what was to come, her mother wrote to *The Times* newspaper questioning the ethics of the Press in hounding her daughter.

ABOVE:
*Earl Spencer
with his second
wife, Raine.*

21

OPPOSITE:

A pensive Diana a month before her engagement was announced.

LEFT:

Diana begins to blossom in the limelight.

DIANA
And Charles

❧ AS THE RELATIONSHIP BETWEEN CHARLES AND DIANA
BLOSSOMED, IT BECAME CLEAR BY THE BEGINNING OF 1981
THAT IT WAS A QUESTION OF WHEN NOT WHETHER CHARLES
WOULD ASK DIANA TO MARRY HIM ❧ OVER THE PRECEDING
CHRISTMAS HOLIDAY THE COUPLE HAD TENTATIVELY
DISCUSSED THE PROSPECT OF MARRIAGE ❧

iana was known to have had no previous lover – an unspoken
but necessary requirement of becoming the wife of the heir to
the throne. No formal proposal came until February 1981. It
has been suggested since, though not of course at the time, that the Prince's
father, the Duke of Edinburgh, urged his son to speed up the process. When
the proposal *was* finally made Diana needed no time to decide. As she said
later: "It wasn't a difficult decision. It is what I want."

It was what the country wanted too. Prince Charles – thirty-two years of
age though seeming older than his years – had chosen a beautiful, bright
young woman to be his bride, his Princess and, as we all believed then, his
Queen. On February 24, the announcement of the engagement came from
Buckingham Palace and a wedding date was set – July 29. The couple presented themselves for public inspection and showed off the ring – a huge
sapphire surrounded by diamonds. Lady Diana Spencer – as she would
remain for a mere five more months – was facing up to a life she could hardly

OPPOSITE:
*Diana and
Charles pose for
the world as their
engagement is
announced.*

have imagined. At twenty years of age, a young woman with no real experience of public life was taking her first tentative steps into royalty and into an incredibly daunting role. She said she thought that she could cope if she had the Prince alongside her. Later she would reflect that she had been totally unprepared for the rigours of such a way of life. She was clearly in love with Charles but was he in love with her? He said he was – whatever being in love meant. Words that would come to haunt him.

The months between engagement and wedding were hectic, often exhilarating, and sometimes trying. Diana had to learn the restrictions of royal life: never again would she be able to walk quietly to the shops or visit her friends unannounced. Prince Charles had to keep to the schedule he had accepted before the announcement of the engagement, which meant some separation and some tears on Diana's part. She had to accept the absences – a hard lesson so soon after the joy of setting a date – and did her best to hide her feelings. Already Diana was a hit with the crowds wherever she went and as always, she enjoyed meeting children. She made regular trips to see her wedding dress being made and the question of what it would look like became a national obsession. The two young designers she chose to make the dress for her, David and Elizabeth Emanuel, became household names as a result. And like any newly-engaged woman she set about planning the furnishings of their home, or in her case homes: Highgrove in the Cotswolds in western England and their apartments in Kensington Palace. But while the days before the wedding appeared to be happy ones for Diana there was unhappiness too. It was only now that she began to wonder about the relationship between Charles and the woman who had been his first love, Camilla Parker Bowles.

The wedding of the century, as it was called, took place in St Paul's Cathedral in the heart of the City of London. Heads of state from around the world were there to see the first English woman in five centuries marry a

ABOVE:

Diana on her
first public
engagement with
Prince Charles at
Goldsmith's Hall,
March, 1981.

Prince of Wales. Diana prepared herself for her Prince at Clarence House, then the London home of his grandmother, the Queen Mother. She was cheered through the streets by an adoring public as she travelled to St Paul's. When she arrived outside the cathedral in the horse-drawn glass coach, her ivory silk dress, embellished with antique lace and mother-of-pearl sequins, was unfurled behind her, its train twenty-five feet long. The world's biggest television audience at that time watched as Diana's father, Earl Spencer, who

ABOVE:

A word of reassurance from Diana for a nervous bridesmaid.

OPPOSITE:

Diana and her beloved father walk down the aisle at St Paul's Cathedral.

was recovering from a stroke, gave away his daughter. The eyes of the world were on her and she knew it – she looked every inch the beautiful princess that the fairytale script demanded. When the Prince saw her beside him he said: "You look wonderful." "Wonderful for you," was her reply. One minor detail did not go according to that script … the otherwise calm-sounding bride muddled the order of the many names of her husband-to-be during the service. If anything, it made her more endearing. Anyway, at that moment, Diana, a reasonably ordinary girl who had worked at a London kindergarten, became a Princess. Another chapter in the thousand-year history of the British Royal Family had been opened – a Royal Family that would later be changed quite radically by this remarkable young woman.

The couple drove through the streets to Buckingham Palace and delighted the crowds gathered there with a kiss on the balcony. At the end of a day of happiness they drove along the Mall on their way to their honeymoon, the start of a long life together – or so we thought. In Gibraltar, the starting point for the honeymoon, the couple made a brief appearance on the deck of the Royal yacht *Britannia*, before disappearing for two weeks to cruise the Mediterranean, two weeks in which Diana had some time at least to adjust to being the new Princess of Wales. When the couple returned they went back to Balmoral where they had first been spotted together a year earlier. They appeared relaxed, refreshed and ready for the future.

It was right and proper that her first official trip as Princess of Wales should be to Wales itself. The crowds that gathered to greet her symbolized not just her new status but her individual popularity. That was something the Prince appeared to find surprising. Frankly, *he* was used to being the crowd-puller. Soon the royal couple became a royal family of their own. Within a year of their wedding, their first son, William Arthur Philip Louis, better-known to us of course as Prince William, was born. He arrived on June 21, 1982 and, as always with a royal birth, an official notice was placed on the gates of Buckingham Palace. It took a few days for him to be given his very regal string of names: to Diana he would always be simply "Wills". Once more there was reason for the nation to celebrate: Diana had produced an heir for Charles and a future King for her country. The succession was secure and the Royal Family of the twenty-first century was taking shape, thanks to her.

OVERLEAF:

Just married, the beaming couple greet the crowds on their return to Buckingham Palace.

In the spring of 1983 Charles and Diana visited Australia. Prince Charles knew the country well and loved it, but for the Princess it was another new experience and a little bewildering. The Australians, of course, could not get enough of her, nor could the crowds who turned out in New Zealand later in the same trip. In Canada, the same year, it was the same story as the Prince introduced his Princess to the Commonwealth. The Princess's popularity soon became adulation. A new word began to appear in the vocabulary of the media: "Di-mania." Nowhere was that "Di-mania" more in evidence than in the United States, where crowds literally screamed for the Princess wherever she went. They would continue to do so all her life.

Publicly, 1983 was a spectacular year for the Princess, as she became the world's number-one cover girl. All the time, she was growing into her new role and, in public at least, appeared to be carrying it off with ease. She met world leaders she had only ever seen on television and talked to them like friends. Yet occasionally she showed she was still in awe of her own Royal status. The camera caught her collecting a place card with her name on it

ABOVE:

A family celebration to mark Charles Spencer's twenty-first birthday.

OPPOSITE:

The Royal Couple at Kensington Palace.

LEFT:

A traditional carriage ride in Hungary.

TOP LEFT:

Diana and Charles with Princess Grace of Monaco shortly before her death.

TOP RIGHT:

A public display of affection for the polo-playing Prince.

LEFT:

At Ayers Rock on their first official tour to Australia in 1983.

OPPOSITE:

Diana is swept off her feet at a ball in Melbourne.

LEFT:

A playful Diana cracks an imitation bottle over her husband's head on a visit to the Pinewood film studios, 1986.

OPPOSITE:

An official portrait to mark the start of their tour of Australia, 1988.

BELOW:

An audience with Pope John Paul II.

ABOVE:

Smiles in Japan, 1986.

LEFT:

In Australia, 1988.

from a banquet for a souvenir. To the watching world, Charles and Diana seemed at ease with each other – affectionate even – no matter how public the setting. They appeared to be a perfect match and very much in love.

Their second son, Henry Charles Albert David – to be known as Prince Harry – was born on September 15, 1984. Diana had now produced "the heir and the spare." In the two years since William's birth Diana had matured, becoming more relaxed and confident both as a princess and as a mother. The Di-mania continued and on one occasion Prince Charles famously joked that if he could, he would like to be able to divide Diana in two so she could shake hands with people on both sides of a crowded street. Side-by-side their public engagements never failed to attract a worldwide following. While Charles might have been publicly proud of his wife, privately he was still startled by this adulation – perhaps even jealous.

LEFT:

Listening attentively to her husband at the Braemar Highland Games in 1985.

BELOW:

Mixing charity and music at the Live Aid pop concert in 1985.

Other problems were now becoming clear. Diana fainted during a visit to an exhibition in Vancouver, Canada in May 1986. She had been looking thin for some time and only much later was it revealed that the Princess was suffering from the eating disorder bulimia nervosa – a complaint often caused by stress. During 1987, rumours over marital difficulties spread as more and more of their duties were carried out individually. Prince Charles visited woodlands in Cornwall in southwest England on the same day as the Princess presented a pennant to Hussar soldiers a couple of hundred miles away in Hampshire. Not in itself unusual except that it was the couple's sixth wedding anniversary. They were reunited briefly in Scotland but the Princess returned to London while the Prince stayed where he was. The couple had been apart for a month before they were together again for a visit to Wales to meet the victims of floods there earlier in the year. After a few hours together Prince Charles went back to Scotland. The lack of togetherness was plain to see when Prince William suffered a depressed fracture of the forehead after an accident with a golf club. The Princess went in the ambulance with William to London's famous hospital for children, Great Ormond Street, while Charles followed behind in his car. When the operation on William was

ABOVE:

Charles and Diana at the wedding of Prince Andrew to Sarah Ferguson in 1986.

LEFT:

The start of a skiing holiday in Klosters, a favourite royal resort.

over, Charles left for another engagement. It was the Princess who took her son home the next day. The Prince was also absent for Diana's thirtieth birthday celebrations.

By now, British newspapers were calling the marriage "a cause for concern," especially as it seemed Prince Charles had offered his wife a party and she had turned it down. However, during times of trouble there were still some signs of mutual support. In 1992, they were both on holiday skiing in Klosters in Switzerland – a popular destination for the Royals – when the Princess received unexpected and tragic news. Her beloved father had died after appearing to recover from a long period of illness. The funeral for the Earl was held in the tiny village of Great Brington, in Northamptonshire, near the Althorp Estate – the village that was to see so much more grief when Diana herself died only five years later. At Earl Spencer's funeral Diana showed composure and control and Prince Charles was briefly back at her side.

BELOW:

On the slopes in Klosters with the Duke and Duchess of York.

LEFT:

*Guests of Honour
at a traditional
Arabic feast in
Abu Dhabi, 1989.*

The Princess concentrated on her charity work and an endless round of official engagements that helped hide much personal misery. Diana later claimed that no one had prepared her for the job she had to do. The whispers of trouble continued but the full story burst into the open with the publication of a book by Andrew Morton with which, through friends, Diana co-operated. Morton's book included revelations about her husband's relationship with Camilla Parker Bowles, which had started before his marriage. The book caused headlines throughout the world with its claims that the Princess was unhappily married and also that she had tried to kill herself. Whatever else it proved, Morton's book showed that something was definitely wrong with the Wales's marriage. And if anything, it won Diana yet more sympathy from the public.

The Prince became a solitary figure both publicly and privately. But the starkest pictures of isolation were those

RIGHT:

Once again the centre of attention on a trip to Nigeria in 1990.

CENTRE:

A rare chance for public laughter as a comedy sketch is performed in Cameroon.

FAR RIGHT:

Diana arrives in Hungary for a visit in 1990.

of the Princess at the Taj Mahal in India in 1992, a place where Prince Charles had promised to take her. Instead he went to another engagement. They were images of loneliness and despair in a faltering marriage. The Press made much of the solo visit and the Princess's apparent lack of concern over her husband's absence. She enigmatically called the trip a "healing experience," telling reporters to work out what she meant by this for themselves. On the same Indian trip, the world saw the Princess avoid a kiss from her husband after a polo match. It was evident this was a very unhappy couple. On the couple's next foreign trip – to Egypt – the Princess was again alone for much of the time. Once more, she posed alone in front of a famous landmark, the Pyramids, and seemed to be inviting speculation about the relationship. Charles had travelled to Egypt with his wife but then carried on to an archaeological dig in Turkey. On a trip to Korea in late 1992 the body language and the eye contact – or lack of it – could not have made things much clearer. Some say it was during this tour that the couple decided to separate.

The announcement that no-one wanted to hear but many had expected came in December 1992. The fairytale marriage was over. The British Prime

Diana and Charles visit a war cemetery in May 1991 with the Czech president, Vaclav Havel.

Minister John Major formally announced that the couple were to separate and Prince Charles moved out of their shared apartments in Kensington Palace. After the announcement, Diana made it clear her charity work would continue. She addressed a conference called to discuss eating disorders, bravely confronting her own bulimia in public. That part of her life was no longer a secret, but the Press continued to pry and there were secretly recorded tapes in abundance. First there was "Dianagate," supposedly a conversation between the Princess and a male friend she called "Squidgy". Then came "Camillagate", said to be a recording of a conversation between the Prince and Camilla Parker Bowles. Finally, there were the "Highgrove tapes", purporting to be recordings of an argument between the Prince and Princess at their country home.

Diana with her husband, Prince Harry and other members of the Royal Family, 1990.

LEFT:

Laughter for Diana and Prince Edward on their way to an official function, 1993.

RIGHT:

A happy moment with Sarah Ferguson, 1991.

BELOW:

Sharing a joke with her sister-in-law, Princess Anne, 1992.

OVERLEAF:

Looking up at a flypast of Tornado jets during the celebrations to mark the end of the Gulf War, June, 1991.

In November 1993 pictures of her working out in a London gym were printed by a British newspaper. The pictures had been taken with a hidden camera and for Diana they were the final straw. Hurt and wounded, she announced that she was withdrawing from public life. She made her unexpected statement at a charity event at the start of December 1993, cancelling planned foreign trips to Russia and Japan. Most dramatically she said she was scaling back on the number of charities she would support, declaring that she would concentrate on just a few. Close to tears, she explained her reasons:

When I started my public life twelve years ago, I understood that the media might be interested in what I did. I realized then that their attention would inevitably focus on both our public and private lives. But I was not aware how overwhelming that attention would become, nor the extent to which it would affect both my public duties and my private life in a manner that has become hard to bear ... my first priority will continue to be our children, William and Harry, who deserve as much love and attention as I am able to give. I would like to add that this decision has been taken with the full understanding of the Queen and the Duke of Edinburgh who have always shown me kindness and support.

Her most moving remarks came at the end of the speech:

I hope you can find it in your hearts to understand and give me the time and space that has been lacking in recent years. I could not stand here today and make this kind of statement without acknowledging the heartfelt support I have been given by the public. Your kindness and affection have carried me through some of the most difficult periods, and always your love and care have eased the journey.

For those of us at the event, her words caused consternation. Many more surprises were in store as Diana struggled to reconcile her understandable enjoyment of attention with her fear of constant prying by the Press. The Princess did try to create for herself a more private life, but without the all encompassing royal protection it proved hard for her to lead the normal existence she craved. She and Charles continued to make headlines. In June 1994,

OPPOSITE:
Dark days for Diana in 1992 as she and Charles attend the funeral of her father.

57

OPPOSITE:

Unaccompanied by Charles, Diana is shown the marvel of the ancient Sphinx, in Egypt, 1992.

LEFT:

Diana and Charles at a welcoming ceremony in Toronto, 1991.

ABOVE:

Strain takes its toll, Korea, 1992.

RIGHT:

Diana arrives alone at Westminster Abbey, 1992.

in a television interview, the Prince admitted adultery. The night he did so, the Princess was not watching: she was at a charity event wearing a fetching black dress and looking gorgeous, her response to his public admission of unfaithfulness to the woman considered by many to be the most beautiful in the world.

Formal divorce could not now be far away. Before it happened, Diana wanted the public to hear her side of the story. She too did a television interview in which she admitted having had a love affair with James Hewitt, a former Army captain. She also spoke of there being "three of us" in her marriage – the third person being Camilla Parker Bowles – and described her marriage as "a bit crowded". The most damning moment was when she doubted Charles's desire to be King. And she used a phrase already being used to describe her. Yes, she did want to be the "Queen of People's Hearts." Pressure for a divorce in the end came from the Queen. Concerned, and wishing to end the uncertainty, she wrote to the couple telling them to take the final step. The Princess agreed the marriage was over. The divorce came through in July 1996. She received a large financial settlement and was to remain at Kensington Palace. But she was to give up the style, Her Royal Highness, and become instead, Diana, Princess of Wales.

DIANA
The Devoted Mother

✿ DIANA RETAINED MANY OF THE TRAPPINGS OF ROYALTY ✿ BUT LIKE MOTHERS THE WORLD OVER, DIANA'S CHILDREN, WILLIAM AND HARRY, WERE HER OVERRIDING CONCERN ✿ AS ONE FRIEND OF DIANA'S IS REPORTED TO HAVE SAID, "HER SONS WERE HER LIFE" ✿

When she was a child Diana grew up without her own mother at home. As a mother herself, she wanted William and Harry to have the happiness that she felt she had missed out on. Neither Diana nor Charles had liked boarding school and Diana wanted her children to have a family life in their early years. A compromise was decided by the couple. The boys would go to boarding schools, as was traditional in both the Spencer and Windsor families, but they would be schools close to home.

Diana had a very close relationship with her sons and she had clear ideas of how she wanted them to grow up. She wanted them to have as normal a life as possible – to stay in touch with ordinary people. As the mother of the future King, she was also well aware of their responsibilities as young Princes and she was fully aware of the roles they would have to play in later life. Diana wanted to share in the shaping of those roles. It was a huge responsibility – especially for a woman who already felt she was taking on the establishment in carving out a significant place for herself. Diana was a

OPPOSITE:

With her beloved boys, William and Harry in 1990.

ABOVE:

The world catches

its first glimpse of

Prince William

outside St Mary's

Hospital in

London.

modern woman brought up outside the Royal Family. Although she had a privileged upbringing in some senses, the way she wanted to raise William and Harry was always going to be rather different from the manner in which previous princes had been treated. There was no clearer sign of how the Princess wanted to do things differently than on the 1983 Royal trip to Australia and New Zealand. William was not yet a year old but Diana was keen that he should be present on the trip with her and her husband and to prove the point she showed him off. It was on this visit that Prince William gave *his* first real performance for the cameras.

Whatever else was going on in Diana's life, she always made time for William and Harry. She was there for their first days at kindergarten; she

LEFT:

Charles and Diana at William's christening, August 1982.

ABOVE:

The adoring parents admire their first-born.

LEFT:

William performs for the cameras in New Zealand, 1983.

LEFT:

A family photocall on the deck of Britannia, *1985.*

took them on foreign holidays; she kicked off her shoes at their school sports days to take part in – and win – the mothers' race; she took them to Thorpe Park, a theme park outside London; she had satellite television installed at Kensington Palace so the boys could watch their favourite films when they were with her; and she allowed them to play computer games. Whatever their personal differences, Charles and Diana were always very civilized with one another where the children were concerned. Diana and Charles put their arguments aside for William's first day at Eton, the famous school near Windsor, and at subsequent parents' days.

BELOW:

With William in 1984.

The boys had nannies when they were younger and Diana did worry about losing out in their affections as a result. The first was Barbara Barnes who was perhaps too liberal even for Diana. She was followed by Ruth Wallace who was credited with succeeding where Nanny Barnes was said to have failed. Diana also worried about the place in their lives of Tiggy Legge-Bourke, a former nanny who Prince Charles employed to help him with the boys after the separation. One particular incident that was alleged to have upset Diana was William's invitation to Tiggy to join him for a families' picnic at Eton. Diana later issued a

OPPOSITE:

Diana presents Charles and the nation with a second son, Harry, in 1984.

67

OPPOSITE:

An early duet from Princes William and Harry in the drawing room at Kensington Palace.

LEFT:

A family portrait outside their Gloucestershire home.

RIGHT:

Precious moments at home with William.

RIGHT:

William is quick to spot the camera.

BELOW:

William enjoys a carriage ride with his mother and great-grandmother, 1987.

LEFT:

Diana helps William on the way to his first day at school, 1987.

BELOW:

At home at

Highgrove in 1986.

ABOVE:

On Harry's first

day at kinder-

garten, 1987,

the three Princes

compete to shake

the hand of his

new headmistress.

RIGHT:

William, led by

Diana, on his pony

Smoky at

Highgrove.

LEFT:

A tender moment for Diana and Prince Harry.

ABOVE:

*A cuddle for
Harry.*

RIGHT:

*A family holiday
in Majorca, 1987.*

LEFT:

With the boys in Majorca.

LEFT:

A relaxed family photograph on holiday in the Scilly Isles.

TOP LEFT:

On their bikes in
the Scilly Isles,
1989.

BOTTOM LEFT:

A champion mum,
Diana wins her
race at a school
sports day, 1989.

ABOVE:

Off to school in
1989.

statement to make clear that she had not been upset at all. She added that she understood William's wish that the picnic should not become yet another media circus.

It has been said that Diana came to lean on William, discussing her problems with him and making him old before his time. But those who know the boys well believe that all she was doing was informing William of what was going on in her life – she would never have burdened him with her troubles. By this stage, both boys were perhaps already starting to show the contradictory sides of their mother's personality. Harry was said, by those who knew him at the time, to be "a charmer," "a flirt," and "good fun". William was said to be quite shy and more sensitive. He has also found it more difficult than Harry to deal with the attention of the media. But William was developing normal teenage tastes: loud music and designer clothes.

ABOVE:

A trip to Niagara Falls, 1991.

TOP LEFT:
1991 and a skiing holiday for the Princes and their mother.

BOTTOM LEFT:
Diana embraces William on board **Britannia.**

Diana's achievements in modernizing the monarchy are perhaps as clear in the way she treated her sons as in any other aspect of her royal life. Who can forget the pictures of her running towards her sons on the deck of the Royal Yacht *Britannia* on a trip to Canada, when she and Prince Charles had travelled separately from their sons? Diana kissed them and hugged them hard. Motherly love could hardly be clearer. Contrast that scene with similar situations a generation earlier. When Diana's mother-in-law, the Queen, returned from foreign travel, she would greet a young Prince Charles with a handshake.

William and Harry were truly the cornerstones of Diana's life. So much so, it was wanting to be near them that kept her in Britain, when other parts of the world without such intrusive media and with tougher privacy laws, often seemed to her more appealing.

OPPOSITE:

William wins Diana's attention at Wimbledon, 1991.

ABOVE:

Enjoying a sleigh ride through Lech in Austria, 1993.

RIGHT:

Diana guides William through his first official engagement, 1991.

LEFT:

Diana and the Princes meet movie stars Robin Williams and Dustin Hoffman at the Royal Premiere of Hook, 1992.

OVERLEAF:

Diana and the boys with Prince Charles and other members of the Royal Family on VJ Day, 1995.

RIGHT:

All the fun of the fair at Thorpe Park, 1991.

LEFT:

The family watch a march past on the Mall to mark the fiftieth anniversary of VJ day.

RIGHT:

Diana points William in the right direction on his first day at Eton, 1995.

No shortage of interest for William's arrival at Eton College.

LEFT:

The family together for the VE Day celebrations in Hyde Park, 1995.

DIANA
Queen of Hearts

❧ TO UNDERSTAND DIANA'S OWN NEED TO BE THE "QUEEN OF PEOPLE'S HEARTS" IS TO GRASP SOMETHING OF HER APPEAL ❧ SHE WAS GLAMOROUS BUT QUITE PREPARED TO GET HER HANDS DIRTY ❧ OUTWARDLY CONFIDENT BUT INWARDLY INSECURE ❧

Diana saw a real opportunity to do good throughout her life when others in her position might have been satisfied with a comfortable lifestyle and two healthy sons. It was that insecurity which seemed to drive her on. As she grew in confidence, Diana realized that she could use her fame and her influence to make people's lives better.

Diana was, as those who met her knew, a great giggler, a very human and appealing trait, and she did have what is often described as the "common touch". I shall always remember when I was on the receiving end of some of her good humour. During a lunch at ITN one of my colleagues told her I was a railway enthusiast and she spent the rest of the meal pulling my leg about it. She was dreadfully normal! Fascinated by television, she often talked about her favourite programmes with people she met on her engagements. I shall never forget her asking me, in early 1995, if I knew what had been the most popular television programme on Christmas Day, a couple of weeks earlier. *She* knew it had been the soap opera, *EastEnders*, which she

OPPOSITE:
Diana comforts a sick child at a hospital in Pakistan.

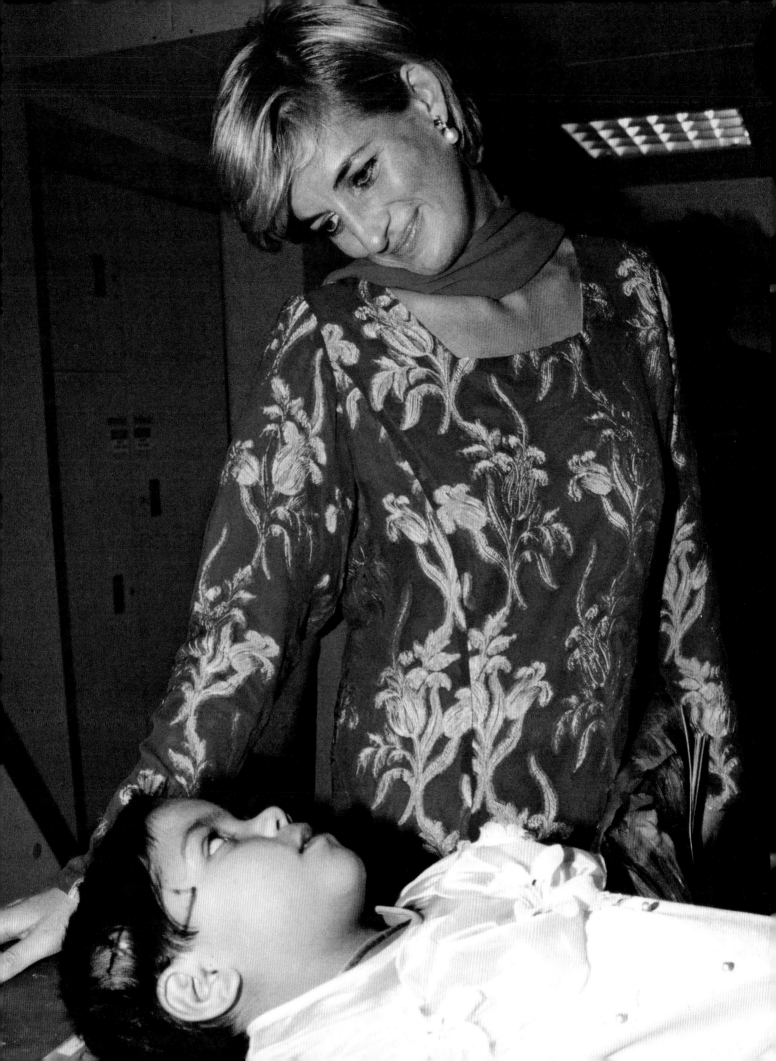

ABOVE:

*Diana attends
a festival of
Remembrance at
the Royal Albert
Hall, 1984.*

had watched, all by herself. A candid and sad admission from the most famous woman in the world that she had been home alone on Christmas Day while her sons were with their father at Sandringham. Her remarks were typical of her honesty and gave a vivid glimpse of her private life. Only someone who is truly lonely can understand how important a kind word, a chat beside a hospital bed, or even a touch of the hand can be. Her friends say she responded to suffering because she had endured much suffering herself: it was a state she knew too well.

Being associated with charities is often part and parcel of being a Royal. In the early days of her public life charities were keen to sign her up. Diana's main interests were with the very young and the very old and those in hospitals or hospices. She told friends that she did not just want to be a name at the top of a piece of headed notepaper. She wanted to do real work – to be "hands on". She did not do it for her own publicity. One charity worker said she never shied away from leaving the appointed route through the hospital ward and – out of sight of the cameras and out of range of the microphones – offering comfort and conversation to someone who perhaps had not expected to meet her. Another said that she had never seen anyone with such an ability to create a rapport with people so quickly. She could approach a group of people who were nervous of meeting a real princess, with all her glitz and glamour, and within moments she would have them relaxed and laughing and joking.

Diana was always willing to meet the less fortunate and give them encouragement. She was patron of Turning Point, an organization that helps people recovering from drug or alcohol addiction,

LEFT:

*Diana, Duchess of
Cornwall, visits a
hospital in
St Austell, 1983.*

88

and she supported work for the homeless. Diana wanted William and Harry to see something of how homeless people lived and took them with her – in private – to meet people sleeping rough on the streets. One highly publicized crusade was to dispel fears of contact with AIDS sufferers and on her many trips to open new wards devoted to their treatment she made a point of shaking hands with, and talking to, patients with the disease.

OVERLEAF:

Diana touches hands and hearts on a tour of Canada, 1986.

Similarly with leprosy, she wasn't afraid to touch – helping to change public attitudes in the process. Drug abuse was another of Diana's concerns and she wanted to be involved in the fight against it. She also showed great concern for the deaf and learned sign language. Not for Diana a few token signs – she could understand and communicate properly, proof of her commitment to her cause.

Her Queen of Hearts role also extended to more conventional royal duties. For example, she boosted the morale of serving soldiers on various postings – routine or dangerous. She was the Colonel-in-Chief of, among others, the Royal Hampshire Regiment and in Canada, The Princess of Wales's Own Regiment. Even in combat gear the Princess managed to look glamorous. During the Gulf War between the Western Allies and Iraq she gave support to the families of servicemen and women fighting in the desert and chatted to soldiers and airmen before they set off. She gave great comfort to many during frightening times. It wasn't just the British forces who idolized her – US troops made her their pin-up too. Diana's charity work often took her to the movies and while she usually enjoyed the films, it was the charitable cause behind the premiere that mattered most.

ABOVE:

Diana on a visit to Bahrain, 1986.

ABOVE:

A visit to brighten a day on a North Sea oil rig, 1985.

LEFT:

Diana gets to grips with an Armoured Fighting Vehicle at the Wavell Barracks, Berlin.

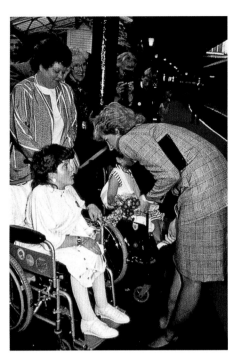

BELOW:

Talking to Buddhist monks at a temple in South Korea, 1992.

ABOVE:

A word of comfort from Diana, 1988.

RIGHT:

Sign language used on a visit to the British Deaf Association.

OPPOSITE:

Terence Donovan's portrait of a Princess.

There were plenty of foreign trips. In 1993 when she went to Zimbabwe with the Red Cross, the idea was not to show images of starving people but to show the charity's success in providing help for people at a feeding station. Without Diana, the picture opportunity would have been nothing. With her, the message of that success was beamed around the world. As friends pointed out, while she was often the victim of the media's unwanted attentions she knew how to use its power for good. Like the Queen Mother, she always knew where the camera lenses were. She was well aware of the pulling power of her image, and was happy for charities around the world to benefit from it. Another good cause to benefit from her support was the cancer hospital in Pakistan that Imran Khan, the former international cricketer and aspiring politician, had founded. Khan married Diana's friend from London, Jemima Goldsmith. Again, powerful and moving images of her

ABOVE:

Diana looking every inch the Princess, 1987.

BELOW:

A warm welcome for Diana in Budapest.

RIGHT:

First Lady Barbara Bush welcomes Diana to the White House, 1990.

RIGHT:

The height of elegance: Diana at the enthronement banquet of Japanese Emperor Akihito, 1990.

BELOW:

Diana displays her gentle touch.

OPPOSITE:

A posy for a Princess on a visit to Somerset, 1991.

LEFT:

Sharing a private confidence on a public visit to an AIDS clinic.

RIGHT:

Diana delights a group of Czech orphans by revealing a hidden talent.

OPPOSITE:

Attending a Concert of Hope on World AIDS Day, December 1, 1993.

ABOVE:

Diana at an advice centre for the homeless in London's King's Cross.

LEFT:

An award to remember for the young victim of a terrorist car bomb attack.

The Princess of Wales inspects her own regiment in Canada, 1991.

holding sick children helped get the donations pouring in. Diana's popularity in the United States in particular made her a must-have guest at many glittery charity events. I have vivid memories of her visit to Chicago in June 1996. Bathed in sunlight, she came down a sweeping staircase to be greeted by one of the most sophisticated yet cynical audiences in the world – and they were completely bowled over by her.

Her short but high-profile association with the Red Cross's anti-landmines campaign brought her praise and controversy. No-one has looked more fetching in a bomb proof vest and visor that she wore during her visit to Angola. But she was straying into a political minefield as well as a real one – some said the issue was just too complex. Not so, replied a testy Diana, declaring that she was a humanitarian figure, not a political one. To prove her point, she took her crusade on to Bosnia.

BELOW:

A night at the
Opera, 1991.

ABOVE:

Diana is made an
honourary Chitral
scout on a visit to
Pakistan.

BELOW:

Glittering in
Pakistan, 1991.

ABOVE:

Time to reflect in
Cairo, 1992.

RIGHT:

A formal welcome to Cairo from the Egyptian President, Hosni Mubarak.

LEFT:

Diana visits Mother Teresa's hospice in Calcutta, 1992.

OPPOSITE:

Young dancers meet their Royal audience at the British School in Seoul, 1992.

LEFT:

The Princess of Wales at a children's centre in East Glamorgan District Hospital.

BELOW:

Chatting with workers at the annual British Deaf Association Conference, Blackpool, 1992.

OPPOSITE:

Diana on a hospital visit, 1992.

OPPOSITE:

Making a wish come true for Jessica Finster, a young leukaemia sufferer who dreamt of meeting a Princess.

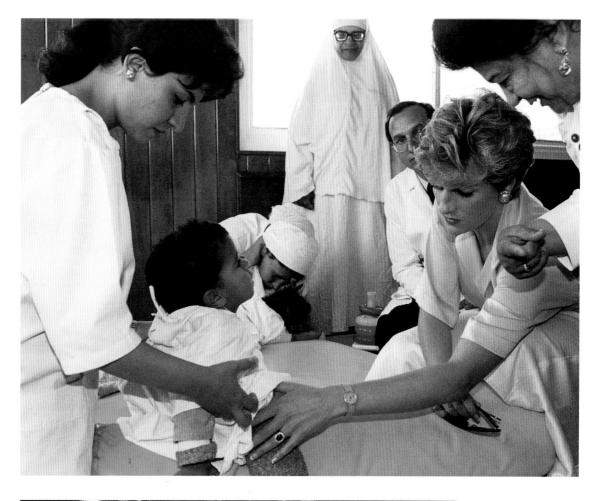

ABOVE:

Diana meets a little boy with polio on her trip to Egypt.

RIGHT:

Listening in at the control tower of London City Airport.

LEFT:

*A box of
chocolates from a
schoolboy admirer.*

BELOW LEFT

AND OPPOSITE:

*A warm welcome to
Nepal, 1993.*

BELOW:

*On a shopping trip
to Paris, 1992.*

OVERLEAF:

*Diana reaches
out to the public
on a walkabout
in South London.*

ABOVE:

A walkabout in the university city of Oxford, 1993.

RIGHT:

At a school in South London.

BELOW:

Taking a closer look on a visit to Cambridge University.

RIGHT:

Sharing a quiet word on a trip to Zimbabwe, 1993.

LEFT:

Inspecting the Princess of Wales's Royal Regiment.

LEFT:

Laying the foundation stone for a new building at Emmanuel College, Cambridge.

LEFT:

A bouquet from a young lady.

Whatever was going on in her private life, every year Diana added more charities to her portfolio. Many were modern organizations dealing with new illnesses and new social problems. But always there were charities associated with children: Barnardo's, Birthright, the Malcolm Sargent Fund for Sick Children, Child 2000, the National Council for Child Health, The National Children's Orchestra, Great Ormond Street Hospital, the Child Accident Prevention Trust, and on and on. By the time of her decision to step back from public life she had a total of 118 charities with which she was associated. When the decision came to part company with more than one hundred of them it was partly to escape the attentions of the media, but also because she wanted to change the direction of her work – to concentrate on a few key areas where she felt she could make most difference. Her friends said it was not a decision she had taken lightly: she needed a rest and she needed

ABOVE:

Diana is entranced by Philip Loft, a three-year-old cancer patient, at the Royal Marsden Hospital, 1993.

OVERLEAF:

Flowers for Diana on her visit to Nepal.

OPPOSITE:

A traditional greeting from Diana on a visit to Nepal, 1993.

RIGHT:
Sharing a private joke at a reception near her Kensington home.

RIGHT:

Diana reports her experience of eating disorders at a conference on the problem, 1993.

ABOVE:

At a gala performance of La Boheme *in aid of the British Red Cross.*

ABOVE:

Signing a photograph at a hospice in Taunton, Somerset.

ABOVE:

Clasping the hand of an anxious admirer.

ABOVE:

Acting as an
ambassador for the
Red Cross at a
child feeding
program in
Zimbabwe, 1993.

time to decide how best to use her undoubted gifts of communication and compassion.

Her role as a fashion ambassador was one she took seriously too. As Lady Diana, in her early days she had dressed like many of her contemporaries from similar backgrounds; pearls and wellington boots featured a good deal. She was the archetypal Sloane Ranger – so named after Sloane Square in London, the fashionable place to live for rich young women. The "look" consisted of patent pumps, Laura Ashley skirts or jeans and a high pie-crust collared blouse with a string of pearls. For the evening, the Sloane Ranger wore yards of taffeta with extraneous bows and flounces and a pearl choker. Within a week or so of the announcement of her engagement, shops began selling "Lady Di" fashions. And when she got married, copies of her Emanuel wedding dress were being made the same day. David and Elizabeth Emanuel

OPPOSITE:

A dazzling Diana
arrives for a gala
dinner at the
Serpentine Gallery
in London's Hyde
Park, 1994.

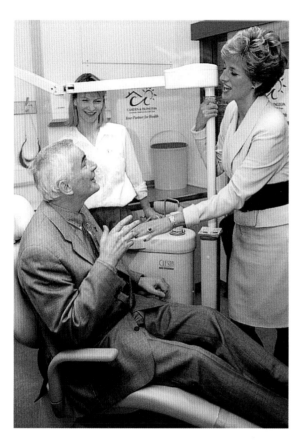

BELOW:

*Enjoying a trip to
New York, 1994.*

ABOVE:

*On a visit to
Europe's biggest
AIDS clinic in
London, 1994 .*

LEFT:

*A word with
a veteran on
the fiftieth
anniversary of
D-Day.*

OPPOSITE:

*A chance to smile
at an official
ceremony in
London's Green
Park.*

LEFT:

Campaigning on behalf of the homeless at London's Centrepoint.

OPPOSITE:

Attending the Concert of Hope in Cardiff.

LEFT:

A visit to a hospital in Buenos Aires.

LEFT:

Teasing a smile during an inspection of British troops in Germany.

RIGHT:

Unveiling a new look at an awards ceremony in the United States.

BELOW:

An intimate moment with Gemma Quinn, a paralysed schoolgirl.

OVERLEAF:

LEFT:

A visit to North London, 1995.

RIGHT:

At the Anglican Cathedral in Liverpool, 1995.

OPPOSITE:
A beaming Diana at a charity dinner in Sydney.

ABOVE AND RIGHT:
Diana at the Pakistan hospital run by Imran and Jemima Khan, 1996.

OPPOSITE:
Diana's favourite press photograph shows her cradling a young cancer victim in Pakistan.

ABOVE:
Gentle applause from Diana at a charity ball in Washington DC 1996.

OPPOSITE:

A wave for the crowds in Chicago.

LEFT:

Visiting the Sacred Heart Hospice in Sydney, 1996.

LEFT:

The centre of attention in Buenos Aires.

RIGHT:

With Jemima Khan in Pakistan.

BELOW LEFT:

With Elizabeth Dole at a gala dinner for land-mine victims in Washington.

BELOW RIGHT:

Visiting a Hindu temple in North London.

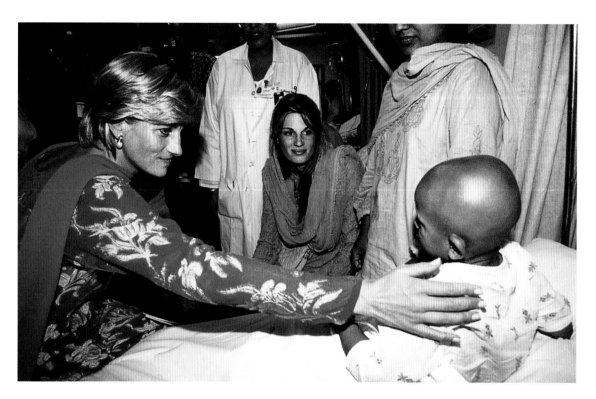

said that when the Princess first came to them she was a chubby, normal, nursery school teacher, bubbly but a little shy. Yet she started a new romantic era in women's clothing. Many designers, said Elizabeth Emanuel, owed their entire careers to Diana, who began to sport a style of her own. Its changes reflected those going on in her life and her tastes matured as she did. At first she was quite daring. There were occasional mistakes: she was criticized by the Italian press – and they know a thing or two about fashion – in 1985 for what she wore on her tour there.

Often Diana was able to combine her charity work with her interest in fashion. She attended fashion shows to raise money in Britain and around the world. She was a regular at British fashion week and fashion awards ceremonies. She was British fashion's greatest export. Catherine Walker was perhaps her favourite designer, but there were countless other designers based in Britain and from abroad that Diana commissioned: Amanda Wakeley, Caroline Charles, Bruce Oldfield, Christina Stambolian, Tomasz Starzewski, Chanel, Donna Karan, Jacques Azagury, Louis Feraud, Escada, to name but a few. Her favourite shoemakers? Manolo Blahnik, Jimmy Choo and Gino Shoes.

Perhaps Diana's ultimate intertwining of fashion and charity came only two months before her death: the sale in New York of seventy-nine of her gowns. All had memories, many of them happy. But here was a marvellous opportunity

LEFT:

Diana surrounded by children at the Shri Swaminarayan Mandir Hindu Temple.

Be my Valentine: a patient at Great Ormond Street Children's Hospital shows Diana his appreciation.

LEFT:

Smiles all round at a charity awards ceremony.

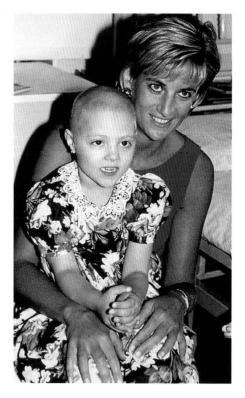

RIGHT:

Secure in the arms of a Princess.

OPPOSITE:

A radiant Diana steps out for a gala evening in London.

RIGHT:

The cost of war:
Diana surveys the
destruction of
Kuito in Angola.

RIGHT:

Diana cuddles a baby at the Kikolo Health Post in the Angolan capital Luanda.

FAR RIGHT:

Wearing a bomb-proof visor during a visit to a mine-field in Angola.

LEFT AND
BOTTOM LEFT:
Diana's visit to Angola boosted her campaign against landmines.

to raise millions for charity. She knew that as items for auction, the dresses would be far more valuable to cancer and AIDS research than they would be to her. The idea for the auction came from her fifteen-year-old son, William.

Another of her favourite designers was, of course, Gianni Versace. He was shot dead outside his home in Miami only a few weeks before Diana herself died. Who can forget that powerful image of Diana as she comforted the singer Sir Elton John, like her, a friend of the designer, at Versace's memorial service. Who would have thought Sir Elton would be at another such service later in the summer – the funeral of Diana.

PREVIOUS PAGE
AND RIGHT:
*Diana in Bosnia
to meet landmine
victims there.*

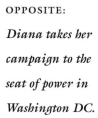

OPPOSITE:

Diana takes her campaign to the seat of power in Washington DC.

LEFT:

Supporting the troops working in Bosnia.

BELOW:

Chatting with two young mine victims.

DIANA
And Friends

✽ DIANA'S FRIENDSHIP WITH SIR ELTON JOHN WAS LIKE MANY OF HER FRIENDSHIPS – COMPLICATED AND INTERMITTENT ✽ THERE WAS SAID TO HAVE BEEN A FALLING OUT AT SOME POINT ✽ YET SHE WAS THERE FOR HIM DURING THE VERSACE SERVICE, WHEN HE NEEDED, LITERALLY, A SHOULDER TO CRY ON ✽

Another complicated and certainly more publicized friendship was that with Sarah Ferguson, who became Duchess of York when she married Prince Andrew. The two young women certainly seemed to have much in common: both married into the Royal Family, and both were involved in much controversy. As new members of the family "firm" they had a lot to learn. On one occasion the two young women were said to have dressed up as policewomen for a night out – and nobody recognized them. The two royal couples went skiing together and posed happily on the slopes, although Prince Charles looked a little less than pleased when Diana and Sarah began pushing one another over in the snow.

When Diana died, Sarah spoke of Diana as her sister, not literally, but in her heart; however, in reality their relationship had cooled. Diana was said to have been upset by comments attributed to her sister-in-law in her autobiography. Also Diana had learned to be royal in a way that Sarah never matched. The Princess needed to be able to insulate herself from

RIGHT:

Diana with Sir Paul McCartney, one of her many friends in the pop music world.

156

Sarah's more outrageous behaviour and a rather distant friendship was the result.

A lot of Diana's friendships were with the rich and famous, many of whom she met at charity events and on public engagements. They could get close to her in a way that other people could not, because through their own experiences, they knew something of her life and its pressures. The mourn-ers at her funeral included a line up of superstars: people such as Sir Elton John, Tom Cruise and Nicole Kidman, Tom Hanks, Steven Spielberg, Luciano Pavarotti, George Michael and Sting. Yet she was a bigger star than any of them.

Just after Diana's death, her friend Rosa Monckton gave a rare television interview to ITN. The Princess was godmother to Rosa's daughter Domenica, a Down's Syndrome child born in 1995. Rosa Monckton described Diana as a complete stalwart, who had stood by her in difficult

RIGHT:

Diana with Sarah Ferguson. They often sought comfort in each other's company.

LEFT:

Diana chats with her friend George Michael before a concert to mark World AIDS Day, 1993.

times. Diana supported her, let her rant and rave, and said she would be there for her. As a friend she was both loving and constructive. She had compassion – and not the kind which could be switched on and off but genuine feelings which came from the heart. When asked what she would remember about Diana's friendship, Rosa Monckton replied: "Her enormous kindness and also her sense of fun. And an incredible inner strength."

And what are we to make of that final friendship in Diana's life – her romance with Dodi Fayed? It seemed to catch everyone by surprise. Dodi's family and Diana's had known each other for many years. When news broke that Diana was on holiday with the Al Fayed family no mention was made of any relationship with Dodi, usually described as a playboy, who was heir to the Harrods empire. There were no romantic overtones; the Princess and her sons were simply holidaying with old friends in the South of France. It was only when Diana reappeared with Dodi on another holiday – this time in Sardinia – that the rumours started to fly. Diana herself told her friend Rosa Monckton she was "blissfully happy". She certainly looked like a woman in love.

RIGHT:

A day out with friends at the Stella Artois tennis championships at London's Queen's club.

BELOW:

With the tennis player Virginia Wade and singer Cliff Richard.

LEFT:

*Arm in arm with
the opera singer
Luciano Pavarotti.*

RIGHT:

*Diana laughs with
her friend Aileen
Getty, who has
fought AIDS for
many years.*

LEFT AND
PREVIOUS PAGE:
*In Pakistan with
her close friend
Jemima Khan.*

RIGHT:
*Mother Teresa
had a profound
influence on
Diana's life.*

ABOVE:
*Dancing the night
away with John
Travolta at the
White House.*

LEFT:

Diana shares her love of dancing with her friend Wayne Sleep.

LEFT:

A friend from the film world. Diana and Lord Attenborough.

ABOVE:

Diana's charm and compassion won her many admirers, including Henry Kissinger.

TOP LEFT:

Diana comforting Sir Elton John at the funeral of their mutual friend Gianni Versace.

TOP RIGHT:

The fashion industry embraced Diana, seen here with Calvin Klein and Donna Karan.

ABOVE:

Diana shared many concerns with Hillary Clinton.

LEFT:

Diana was said to have been blissfully happy in her final weeks with Dodi Fayed. They were introduced by his father Mohamed Al Fayed, the Harrods boss.

DIANA
Goodbye England's Rose

❧ DIANA DIED AS SHE HAD LIVED – HUNTED BY THE PAPARAZZI – AND IN A BLAZE OF WORLDWIDE ATTENTION ❧ THE MOST GLAMOROUS WOMAN IN THE WORLD SUFFERED FATAL INJURIES IN A HORRIFIC CAR ACCIDENT IN A DARK UNDERPASS IN PARIS ❧

The end of Diana's life will remain in all our memories. Like the death of President Kennedy for other generations, everyone will recall the moment they heard the news. My phone rang at around 1.30 in the morning London time and I knew it had to be bad news. My first thought was that one of my children had been in an accident. On the other end of the line, an ITN colleague told me what was known then: Diana and Dodi had been in a car crash in Paris and Dodi was dead. Diana was known to be injured but it was not clear how seriously. Like millions of other people I could not believe what I was hearing. I hurried into work and it was only after we went on the air that word came through that Princess Diana, the woman who so many hoped would have made such a wonderful Queen had circumstances been different, had died. I was reporting the events, yet still spent most of the day disbelieving what had happened. It was the worst experience I have had in journalism. I knew that we were bringing the world the most terrible news.

ABOVE:

A prayer for Diana amid the tributes outside Kensington Palace.

Through that morning in Britain, people were waking up to what had happened. Even those who were not particular fans of the Princess shed tears that day. Remembrances and tributes to her flooded in from all over the globe from friends, heads of state, politicians and the people she had worked so tirelessly for.

Nothing could have prepared us for the way she died. Nor could anything have prepared us for what followed. Flowers began to appear outside the royal palaces in London, and at other places associated with Diana's life. The trickle of tributes became a flood, then great oceans of colour. The first morning, the world watched as her two sons went to the small church near Balmoral where they had been staying as their school summer holiday drew to a close. We listened as Diana's brother, bereaved and angry, attacked the media for its part in his sister's death. Later we watched as Prince Charles left Balmoral, and with Diana's two sisters, flew to Paris where he visited the hospital in which the staff had fought to save the Princess. Her former husband accompanied Diana's coffin home. Just before seven that Sunday evening, the Royal Plane returned to Diana's homeland with its precious cargo wrapped in a Royal Standard. Prince Charles then flew back to Balmoral to be with his – and her – sons at the end of an impossibly difficult day.

That night I reported live from Kensington Palace. As I faced the camera, behind me hundreds of people had gathered. As I reported, it had already become a place of pilgrimage –

BELOW:

Earl Spencer reacts to his sister's death with sorrow and anger.

Britain's Prime Minister, Tony Blair, perhaps summed up the feelings of millions around the world. This is what he said on the morning of Diana's death.

I FEEL LIKE EVERYONE ELSE IN THIS COUNTRY TODAY, UTTERLY DEVASTATED. OUR THOUGHTS AND PRAYERS ARE WITH PRINCESS DIANA'S FAMILY, IN PARTICULAR HER TWO SONS. OUR HEARTS GO OUT TO THEM. WE ARE TODAY A NATION IN A STATE OF SHOCK, IN MOURNING THAT IS SO DEEPLY PAINFUL FOR US. SHE WAS A WONDERFUL AND WARM HUMAN BEING. THOUGH HER OWN LIFE WAS OFTEN SADLY TOUCHED BY TRAGEDY SHE TOUCHED THE LIVES OF SO MANY OTHERS IN BRITAIN AND THROUGHOUT THE WORLD WITH JOY AND COMFORT. HOW MANY TIMES WILL WE REMEMBER HER IN HOW MANY DIFFERENT WAYS WITH THE SICK, THE DYING, THE CHILDREN AND THE NEEDY? WHEN WITH JUST A LOOK OR A GESTURE THAT SPOKE SO MUCH MORE THAN WORDS, SHE WOULD REVEAL TO ALL OF US HER DEPTH OF COMPASSION AND HER HUMANITY. PEOPLE EVERYWHERE LIKED PRINCESS DIANA. THEY LOVED HER. THEY REGARDED HER AS ONE OF THE PEOPLE. SHE WAS THE PEOPLE'S PRINCESS AND THAT IS HOW SHE WILL REMAIN, IN OUR HEARTS AND OUR MEMORIES FOR EVER.

LEFT:

Charles and Diana's sisters arrive at RAF Northholt.

there were people of all ages. There were many children. The odd thing was how quiet it was. I could hear the noise of the London traffic but from the people in the park, almost nothing. What the television audience could not really see in the darkness were the flowers – masses and masses of them, lining the railings, around trees, up to the golden gates of the Palace. The building itself had a forlorn air. There were no lights on in the windows – they looked like big, blank, unseeing eyes. Two images have stuck in my mind from that day. One was the first horrific sight of Diana's mangled car. The other was her coffin returning by plane to British soil.

In life, Diana had been like no other Royal. And after her death there was no script to follow, no clear procedure to adhere to. The funeral was eventually set for the following Saturday, September 6. Arrangements began to be made: there was to be a minute's silence across the country; soldiers who would normally follow a Royal coffin would be replaced by 500 members of Diana's favourite charities; Sir Elton John would sing a

LEFT:

Diana's coffin returns home draped in a Royal Standard.

LEFT:

Harry holds fast to his father's hand as he reads tributes to his mother outside Balmoral.

OVERLEAF:

The three Princes surrounded by an ocean of floral tributes outside Kensington Palace.

ABOVE:
*The people
mourned Diana
with more than a
million bouquets
of flowers.*

specially reworked version of his classic song "Candle in the Wind"; a Union Flag atop Buckingham Palace would fly at half-mast. Giant television screens were erected in Hyde Park for the crowds to follow the service. Diana's body would not after all leave for the service at Westminster Abbey from St James's Palace, the London home of her ex-husband, but from Kensington Palace – her own home. And she would be buried on a tree-covered island in a lake on the Althorp Estate, not in the Spencer family's burial plot in the local village churchyard. To get there, the hearse carrying her coffin would have to drive through North London, on to the M1 motorway and so to Althorp Park. In the week that followed her death the flowers continued to be brought to the

BELOW:
*A father's tribute
to Dodi and
Diana at Harrods.*

Palaces, and people queued through the night to sign Books of Condolence at St James's Palace.

The evening before the funeral Diana's body was taken from St James's Palace to Kensington Palace. It was an unprecedented, utterly moving sight. The small procession of shiny black cars drove through streets that were packed twenty or more deep by people wanting to get a glimpse of their Princess. A sunset over Buckingham Palace made a dramatic background as her coffin passed by. Her route was illuminated by a constellation of flash-bulbs and the way was strewn with flowers.

The next morning, the sun shone on the million or so people who took their places on London's roadsides. There was something quite eerie about the moment the gun carriage with Diana's coffin came through the gates at Kensington Palace at ten minutes past nine. The silence was broken by

BELOW:
The Queen and Prince Philip survey the flowers outside Buckingham Palace.

OVERLEAF:
London stands silent as Diana's coffin is borne on a gun carriage to Westminster Abbey.

177

haunting cries of grief. On top of the coffin were three wreaths of white flowers. On the front wreath was an envelope with a card inside: there was just one word on the envelope in boyish handwriting: "Mummy."

From the moment the coffin left Kensington Palace, Diana's home, armfuls of flowers were thrown into its path. As the cortège neared Buckingham Palace, there was another extraordinary sight: the Queen was standing on the pavement outside her home alongside the crowds – her people – watching with them the funeral procession. With her were other members of the Royal Family including her daughter the Princess Royal, her sons Prince Andrew and Edward, and her sister Princess Margaret. There too was the Duchess of York. We expect somehow to see them on the *balcony* of Buckingham Palace, not on the street. A few minutes later it became clear why the Duke of Edinburgh was not with the rest of his family. At St James's Palace he took his place behind the coffin, walking the mile or

ABOVE:

Prince Philip,
Prince William,
Earl Spencer,
Prince Harry and
Prince Charles
join the funeral
procession.

LEFT:

The Union Flag
at Buckingham
Palace flies at
half mast for
the first time.

180

so to Westminster Abbey beside his grandsons, William and Harry, their father, and Diana's brother, Earl Spencer.

The young Princes behind their mother's coffin was another unforgettable and tragic sight: William with his head bowed most of the time, Harry striding more purposefully – slightly ahead of the others – with his head up. At Westminster Abbey the congregation was arriving. There were political leaders past and present, but only a few as Diana's family had wanted there to be plenty of spaces for friends, especially those from the charity world.

LEFT:

Tom Cruise,
Nicole Kidman,
Tom Hanks and
Steven Spielberg
enter the Abbey.

The hymns and music chosen for the service were favourites of Diana's. The crowds outside, watching on television screens, or listening to loudspeakers joined in. Her sisters both gave readings. Sir Elton John somehow managed to keep control of his emotions when others could not as he sang about England's Rose in "Candle in the Wind".

Earl Spencer spoke movingly about his sister's life and passionately about her death. He promised to honour her memory by protecting her sons – her "beloved boys", he called them. And he somehow summed up what we had all been thinking about Diana over the previous week. "She had a natural nobility. She needed no royal title to generate her particular brand of magic. She was unique, complex, extraordinary and irreplaceable."

ABOVE:
A personal wreath from Prince Harry.

LEFT AND OVERLEAF:
Welsh Guards carry Diana's coffin through the Abbey.

OPPOSITE:
The Abbey filled with two thousand mourners for a unique funeral.

HIS MINISTERS
FOR GOD
FOR KING AND COUNTRY
FOR LOVED ONES HOME AND EMPIRE
FOR THE SACRED CAUSE OF JUSTICE AND
THE FREEDOM OF THE WORLD
THEY BURIED HIM AMONG THE KINGS BECAUSE HE
HAD DONE GOOD TOWARD GOD AND TOWARD
HIS HOUSE

ABOVE:

*Diana's coffin
lies between the
Spencers and the
Royal Family.*

In his address, Earl Spencer said the last time he had seen his sister alive was on her thirty-sixth birthday, on July 1. As the Earl said, she was not celebrating her own special day with friends but was a guest at a fund-raising charity event at the Tate Gallery in London. I was there to cover the story. It was the last time I saw her alive too. She looked radiant and happy – the best and the brightest memory I have.

As Diana's coffin left the Abbey there was applause from the crowds. Until that day, clapping at a funeral had not seemed a very British thing to do but the Princess was changing us in death, as she had in life. Seeing the hearse driving through North London along ordinary streets, past shops, petrol stations and

ABOVE:

*Tony Blair reads
the lesson from St
Paul's letter to the
Corinthians.*

LEFT:

*Sir Elton John
bids his farewell to
England's Rose.*

185

ABOVE:
*Earl Spencer
delivers a
passionate tribute
to his sister.*

houses was for me one of the more remarkable memories of the day. And all the time, people kept throwing flowers on to the hearse. There were so many that the driver had to stop at the beginning of the motorway to remove them from his windscreen. All along the M1, crowds watched her last journey. The police turned a blind eye as drivers on the opposite carriageway stopped their cars and climbed out of them to see the funeral pass by.

Eventually Diana's coffin was carried through the small villages of Northamptonshire to her final resting place, that lovely leafy island, covered after the funeral by many of the bouquets, which had been left outside Althorp Park. It seemed an appropriate choice. Diana's burial place has both splendour and loneliness – just as her life did.

RIGHT AND
OPPOSITE TOP:
*Diana's coffin
leaves Westminster
Abbey.*

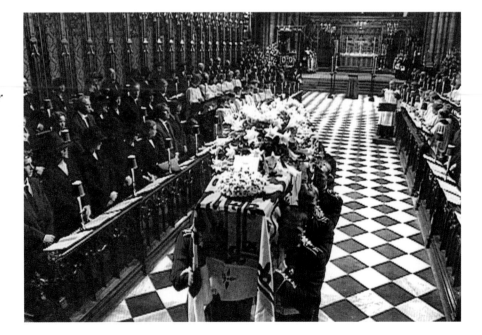

BELOW:

The flower-strewn hearse takes Diana's body to its final resting place at Althorp.

RIGHT:

One of a million tributes to the People's Princess.

RIGHT:

A personal message to the Princess who was mourned by so many as a friend.

BELOW:

Flowers are taken to the peaceful island at Althorp where Diana was laid to rest.

DIANA'S
Legacy

❧ DURING DIANA'S LIFE IT SEEMED SHE HAD CHANGED THE ROYAL FAMILY FOR EVER ❧ TWENTY YEARS AFTER HER DEATH, HER MEMORY IS STILL BRIGHT FOR SO MANY ❧ HER TWO SONS SO OFTEN REMIND US OF THE PRINCESS WE LOST ❧

The world that Diana knew has changed enormously in the twenty years since her untimely end. If she had lived on to 2017, imagine how many "selfie" photographs in which she would have been asked to appear. She would have been tracked on an untold number of mobile phones. No matter how responsible the official media might have promised to be, her every public move would have been even more scrutinized than it was in the 1980s and 90s.

No one, not even the Princess, could have foretold where she would end up living, or with whom, if anyone, she would share her life. Finding the privacy she craved would have been more and more difficult. Even though twenty years have passed, she certainly lives on in the memories of people across the world. Any magazine editor short of a story puts Diana on the front cover, knowing sales will benefit.

If death had not taken her so relatively young, Diana would now be in her mid-fifties and a grandmother twice over. For many, it is through her sons William and Harry that she lives on. Amid all the books and speculation about

OPPOSITE:
Prince William was largely left alone to enjoy his university days at St Andrews. It was during these years that he met Catherine Middleton, who would become his wife.

Diana's life and death, the boys have been her staunchest defenders. Way back on the first anniversary of her death, William and Harry, then aged only 16 and 13, issued a statement thanking everyone for their sympathy and support, adding that their mother would have wanted people to move on. They hoped that she and her memory would be allowed to rest in peace.

The Princes had to grow up quickly without the woman they knew as "mummy" to become the men of the world they are today. For Harry, it meant a career in the army, support for many charitable causes and endless press interest in his choice of girlfriends.

For William, the biggest step was marrying Catherine Middleton in 2011, with brother Harry as best man. The Duke and Duchess of Cambridge have become the object of the sort of fascination with Royals that dominated Diana's life. They share with her the ability to enchant crowds, to mingle and speak to people of all ages – the vast majority of whom lead lives so very different from theirs.

BELOW: *Still they come to honour her memory. In 2016, almost two decades on, tributes were laid at the gates of Kensington Palace.*

Then the children came along. Prince George was born in 2013, and Princess Charlotte two years later. Even very young Royals have duties like no one else. Diana's grandson was photographed early in 2016 for postage stamps to mark the ninetieth birthday of his great-grandmother the Queen, alongside his father and his grandfather, the Prince of Wales. Diana often spoke of her pride in her sons, of her desire to see them take their rightful places in the unique world into which they were born. And she would surely have felt the same for her grandchildren. At the same time she would have sympathized with William, in words that she herself might well have uttered, when he spoke in a television interview about wanting his children "to grow up being a little bit more simple in their approach and their outlook".

BELOW: The unofficial memorial near the Pont de l'Alma tunnel in Paris.

Nothing was ever simple for Diana. The controversies and arguments have continued through two decades. At the entrance to the infamous Pont de l'Alma tunnel where she was fatally injured there is an unofficial memorial to her in the shape of a curious Flame of Liberty. For many years after the

ABOVE: *The opening of the Diana Memorial Fountain united the Spencers and the Royal Family.*

crash, candles were lit close to the accident scene, flowers left, and graffiti in different languages offered up tributes like "our unforgettable Princess".

In the twisting, frankly treacherous four-lane tunnel, the traffic roars by pillar 13, the one hit by the car in which Diana was travelling on that dreadful night in 1997. Two years after the crash came a 6,800-page report by the French authorities compiled from 200 witness statements. The report largely blamed the driver, Henri Paul, who was declared to have been drunk and on anti-depressants. In the UK, an inquest into Diana's death didn't open until six and a half years after her death. Those interviewed by the police included Prince Charles.

There were those who would never accept that Princess Diana died as the result of a horrific car smash. Mohammed Al Fayed, the father of Dodi, was one. He accused British intelligence of being behind the accident in the Paris underpass. He also set up a memorial to Diana in Harrods, the world-famous department store he then owned. Some critics found it tasteless.

Diana's life has been remembered in myriad ways. When the huge crowds I remember so well began arriving at Kensington Palace on the night of her death, most simply brought flowers with them. Some, however, also brought cheques or even cash in envelopes. They wanted something good to emerge from tragedy. They wanted to give something in memory of the woman who had herself given so much. A week later, the Diana, Princess of Wales Memorial Fund was officially registered as a charity. At its peak, around six thousand cheques a day were arriving at the Fund. In ten years, it distributed £140 million (around US$175 million) to causes with which Diana was associated, or to those its organizers believed mirrored her interests.

It was bound to be a tall order setting up a charity from scratch with so much money to take care of. While the Memorial Fund did much good work, there were arguments and recriminations over some of its decisions.

BELOW: *The Diana Memorial Playground in Kensington Gardens has become a wonderful place for children to play.*

195

PART SEVEN

Not everyone approved of the choice of some of the beneficiaries, such as groups for refugees and asylum seekers. And there was considerable unease over the way the Fund and the British government chose a physical memorial to Diana. A statue was thought inappropriate for an icon of the late twentieth century. So a memorial fountain in London's Hyde Park was decided on. The opening ceremony brought together the Royal Family and the Spencers. In the Hyde Park sunshine, the Queen offered warm praise of the daughter-in-law who found it so difficult to fit into Royal life.

There are other memorials in parts of London the Princess knew so well. The Diana Memorial Playground in Kensington Gardens has been described by many as the best part of that parkland. There is a seven-mile walk, charted by 90 plaques set in the ground, that takes you to buildings and locations associated with the Princess. It meanders through St James's

BELOW:

The Spencer family's own memorial on the Althorp estate is the closest the public is allowed to Diana's final resting place.

196

Park, Green Park, Hyde Park and Kensington Gardens. And the walk passes Kensington Palace, Buckingham Palace, Clarence House – now the official home of Diana's former husband, Prince Charles – St James's Palace and the one-time home of Diana's family, Spencer House.

For the twentieth anniversary of Diana's death, there is a new garden at Kensington Palace. And inside the Palace, her home for 15 years, her unrivalled style was remembered in an exhibition that brought together a collection of garments from glamorous evening gowns to chic examples of her working wardrobe.

In Northamptonshire, at the Spencer family's Althorp estate, the Princess's brother established his own memorial. Members of the public pay to enter the estate and take a tour of a visitor centre in which there is an exhibition covering Diana's life and a display of some of her dresses. The

BELOW: *"This event is about all that our mother loved in life," Prince William told the audience of the Concert for Diana at Wembley Stadium, which the Princes organized.*

ABOVE: *A scene from the film* The Queen *in which Helen Mirren portrays an anxious monarch dealing with the aftermath of Diana's death.*

island where she was buried remains private, the exact location of her grave kept secret. At least one former employee complained that the island had become very neglected. A spokesman for the estate said foliage had been allowed to sprawl over the area of her grave to "lend privacy to the Princess's final resting place". Nevertheless, it was announced in 2016 that there would be an extensive redesign of the area of the Oval Lake where she was laid to rest, to honour her memory.

Looking back to the widespread grief felt by so many when Diana died, a film that came out in 2006 caught the period quite accurately. It was *The Queen*, starring Helen Mirren as the monarch so suddenly caught up in such tragic and emotional events. Of course, it was how the scriptwriter, the director, and the cast imagined the way the Queen and her family reacted to what happened. Only a few portrayals were real. Among them, Diana herself was shown as she was in life, thanks to footage from the television archives.

OPPOSITE TOP LEFT: *Sharing a laugh after Prince Harry's passing-out parade at Sandhurst.*

OPPOSITE TOP RIGHT: *Prince Harry follows in his mother's footsteps, meeting landmine victims in Mozambique.*

OPPOSITE BELOW: *Prince Harry on patrol in Helmand Province in Afghanistan.*

In the years that followed her death, lessons were learned from the harassment that the Princess so often suffered. Both her sons were largely left alone to study at Britain's most famous public school, Eton. William went on to university, taking a Geography degree at St Andrews. He and his brother excelled as army cadets at Sandhurst.

For Prince William, the throne beckons, even though it is probably many years in the future. Having left his job as an Air Ambulance pilot in East Anglia, his lot is largely to fulfil a busy Royal diary, as he helps to lighten the workload for the Queen. Harry has had his share of Royal visits, combined with much charity work, often echoing his mother's charitable interests. His projects include Sentebale, a charity dedicated to helping vulnerable children in southern Africa, and charities that help military personnel adapting to life after serious injuries.

For both her sons, the painful memories of what happened to their mother can never be erased. But lives and people have to carry on, and adapt

BELOW: *Another royal wedding. Prince William arrives at Westminster Abbey with his best man, brother Harry.*

OPPOSITE:
Thirty years after his parents' wedding, the second-in-line to the throne marries Catherine. Thousands of people flocked to London to celebrate the Royal couple.

LEFT: *Prince Harry plays volleyball during the launch of the Invictus Games for injured service personnel in the Olympic Park in London.*

BELOW: *Prince George, aged nine months, joins William and Catherine on a three-week official tour of Australia.*

to change. Come 2005, the two of them supported their father when he married Camilla Parker Bowles.

As for Diana's legacy, what will it amount to? She certainly helped to change the image of the Royal Family. Instead of the remoteness of some of its leading figures, there was a young and beautiful woman who had the knack of appealing to what are patronisingly called "ordinary people". They knew that for all her privileges she had to cope as a divorced mother of two adored boys. She made some spectacular mistakes. The problem for her, always, was that any errors of judgement were made in the glare of relentless publicity. So I think it is for her human frailties as well as her stunning achievements that she will always be remembered as "The People's Princess".

ABOVE: *William and Catherine with newborn Princess Charlotte outside the Lindo Wing of St Mary's Hospital.*

RIGHT: *Diana's family together on the balcony of Buckingham Palace during the Trooping the Colour that marked the Queen's 90th birthday in June 2016.*

MEMORIES OF PRINCESS DIANA

BILL CLINTON
FORMER US PRESIDENT

We admired her work for children, for those with AIDS, for discouraging landmines and for the love of her sons. I will always be glad I knew the Princess and will always think of her in strong and positive terms, as will Hillary. We can only hope that her work will go forward and that everyone who can will support her sons.

❧

LUCIANO PAVAROTTI
OPERA SINGER

My heart is full of grief and pain. Diana was the most beautiful symbol of humanity and love for all the world. She touched my life in an extraordinary way. She can never be replaced and I will always remember her with deep joy and love.

❧

DAVID EMANUEL
DRESS DESIGNER

I remember her taking the trouble to send us a hand-written note on her honeymoon thanking us for making her wedding dress. I will always remember her as full of life. She was a great wit, always cracking jokes. We should remember all the love she has given to people around the world.

❧

SIR ELTON JOHN
SINGER

This is the most tragic and senseless death. The world has lost one of its most compassionate humanitarians and I have lost a special friend.

❧

JEMIMA KHAN

She was an amazing and remarkable woman, a loyal friend, and a genuine crusader who did good for others. It is a tremendous loss for the nation but above all my thoughts are with her family and especially with her two sons who have lost a wonderful mother whom they both adored.

❧

SIR RICHARD BRANSON
BUSINESSMAN

Her hard work on so many issues was an inspiration and it is hard to believe she is gone. When my family had a terrible car accident a while ago, the first thing we saw when we got home was a lovely note from Diana. That was typical of her kindness. She was always thinking of other people.

❧

LORD ARCHER
NOVELIST AND POLITICIAN

I remember the first time I saw her, being amazed that she was actually as beautiful as the photographs and then when meeting her that she was as relaxed and easy to talk to as everyone had said.

❧

JOHN GRAY
BRITISH RED CROSS

The Princess of Wales was very special to many people; to people she came into contact with, those who attended the events which help us raise money to support our work.
For fifteen years she gave so much to the British Red Cross and over the last eighteen months in particular Diana gave much of her time to help the victims of anti-personnel mines. We are grateful. We want to say thank you and we will remember her forever.

❧

NELSON MANDELA
FORMER PRESIDENT OF SOUTH AFRICA

She was an ambassador for victims of landmines, war orphans, the sick and the needy throughout the world. She was undoubtedly one of the best ambassadors of Great Britain.

❧

IMPRESSIONS OF THE FUNERAL

WAYNE SLEEP
CHOREOGRAPHER

I think she would have loved it. I was worried there was going to be too much pomp and circumstance and not enough humanity, but it was marvellous. It didn't jar in any way. I felt embarrassed because the British attitude of the stiff upper lip says you don't show emotion, just the kind of thing she was trying to break down.

❧

CHRIS DE BURGH
SINGER/SONGWRITER

It was one of the most extraordinary things I have ever been part of. The most moving moment for me was when Earl Spencer made his tribute and outside we could hear the applause grow and it came through the West Door, up the aisle and everybody started clapping. It made my hair stand on end. It felt like the applause was going all the way up to Diana in her coffin.

❧

1961–1997

PICTURE CREDITS

The publishers would like to thank the following sources for their kind permission to reproduce
the pictures in this book:

Camera Press, Getty Images, ITN, PA Photos, Rex Features & Topfoto